BRISTOL CHANNEL SHIPPING
SHIPPING
The Twilight Years

A Sunday afternoon stroll, with the Docks strangely still and silent, afforded the ideal opportunity to see ships at close quarters. Here, the Indian vessel *Jalavijaya* lies in the Queen Alexandra Dock, Cardiff, in the summer of 1965.

BRISTOL CHANNEL
SHIPPING
The Twilight Years

Chris Collard

TEMPUS

First published 2000
Copyright © Chris Collard 2000

Tempus Publishing Limited
The Mill, Brimscombe Port,
Stroud, Gloucestershire, GL5 2QG

ISBN 0 7524 1740 1

Typesetting and origination by
Tempus Publishing Limited
Printed in Great Britain by
Midway Clark Printing, Wiltshire

Contents

Introduction   7

1.   Newport   9

2.   Cardiff and Penarth   43

3.   Barry and the Bristol Channel Pilots   73

4.   Towards West Wales   91

5.   Trinity House   103

6.   Across the Channel   109

7.   Avonmouth and Bristol   115

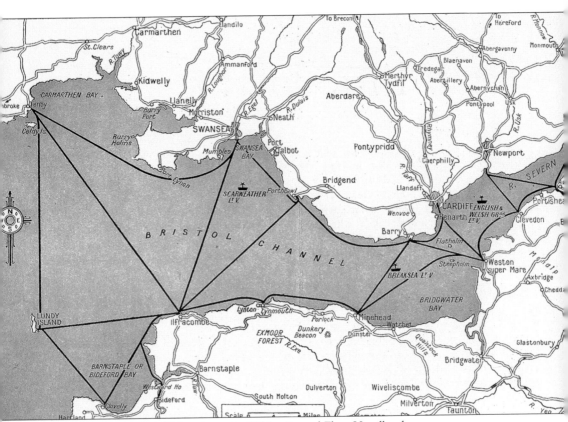

The Bristol Channel. Taken from the White Funnel Fleet Handbook.

Introduction

The present of a camera for Christmas 1954 was the start of my lifelong interest in photography. This, combined with a passion for ships and the sea made me determined to attempt to photograph every ship in the Bristol Channel. However, I soon realized that this plan was totally impracticable, from the point of view of both time and money. School and the limited finances of a nine-year-old do not permit such mammoth undertakings!

Nevertheless, in the early 1960s, when I started work as a channel pilot apprentice with the Newport Pilotage Authority, earning 2 5s 0d per week, photographic material became more financially accessible. Ships became more accessible too. The deck of a pilot cutter was an ideal vantage point from which to 'capture' the great variety of vessels which frequented the Severn Estuary.

My pilot apprenticeship was short lived and was supplanted by the start of a career in photography. However, I continued to record Bristol Channel history from the decks of the White Funnel steamers and on numerous visits to the docks.

Selecting photographs for this book has been a trip down memory lane for me. The main difficulty, however, has been not what to include, but what to leave out from the hundreds of negatives amassed during the early 1960s. Many of those negatives were not printed at the time, as they recorded such ordinary, everyday scenes that I sometimes wondered why I had photographed them at all!

Inevitably, it has not been possible to represent every port and harbour on the shores of the Bristol Channel. It is not intended to diminish the importance of those omitted, but a line has to be drawn somewhere. So I have concentrated on those ports which I visited and photographed most often.

The history of the Bristol Channel ports is long and complex and can only be touched upon here in the very briefest of terms. Bristol itself had been an important maritime centre since medieval times, but it attained particular prominence during the nineteenth century, with the advent of steamships. However, the restricted accommodation and accessibility of the River Avon led to the opening of the first of the Avonmouth Docks in 1877. The South Wales ports thrived during the late nineteenth and early twentieth centuries with the export of coal, brought down by rail from the valleys. In those far off days the channel teemed with shipping of all types – sail and steam, large and small.

Industrial unrest in the 1920s and the depression of the early 1930s brought about a decline at the ports. However, increasing prosperity at the end of the decade, continuing into the early years after the Second World War, revitalized trade in the Bristol Channel ports. From the late 1950s trade waxed and waned as the economy fluctuated, but the 1970s brought about an irrevocable decline.

Nowadays it is becoming rare to see a ship in the Bristol Channel. In the ports, the coal hoists and most of the cranes have gone; the warehouses and transit sheds have been demolished or stand derelict; docks have been filled in. Where commerce once flourished, housing estates now stand.

I am so glad that forty years ago I was 'snap happy' and recorded, unwittingly at the time, the decline of a prosperous waterway.

It is not my intention to overwhelm the reader with a mountain of facts and figures about the ports and their ships, but simply to provide a pictorial journey around the Bristol Channel which, I hope, will bring back memories of the once so common, but long since vanished sights.

One
Newport

Aboard the White Funnel steamer *Glen Usk*, on a family outing from Newport to Ilfracombe, on 8 July 1955. As we left the mouth of the River Usk this rather unusual looking vessel was seen ahead. Her port of registry – Montreal – gave a clue as to her particular line of work.

The ship was the *Manicouagan*, built at the Atlantic Shipbuilding Company's yard on the west bank of the River Usk, for the Q & O Line of Montreal. The vessel was designed for maximum cargo space for carrying wood-pulp and wheat on the Great Lakes of Canada.

Previous page: The Newport Screw Towing Company's tug, *Duneagle*, tows the Houlder Bros. motor-vessel *Swan River* into the South Lock in May 1961.

The *Manicouagan* was being towed into the channel by the Newport Screw Towing Company's tug *Dunson*, to run her trials.

The Pacific Steam Navigation Company's MV *Reina Del Pacifico*, in the south lock on 2 June 1958.

The passenger liner had arrived at Newport in May 1958 and was sold to the shipbreakers, John Cashmore Ltd. In torrential rain she made her final journey to their yard on the River Usk, under her own power, but with the aid of tugs for manoeuvring.

The *Reina Del Pacifico* had been a popular ship on the South American run and was no stranger to the Bristol Channel, having visited Avonmouth on a number of occasions while on troop carrying duties in the Second World War.

The Canadian Pacific Liner, *Empress of France*, dating from 1928, at Cashmore's yard in January 1961. At that time she was the largest ship, in terms of gross tonnage (20,448), to have been broken up at the yard.

The BP tanker, *British Major*, and the destroyer, *HMS Savage*, awaiting demolition at Cashmore's in May 1962.

The Dutch motor-vessel, *Dicky*, at the Baltic Wharf. The wharf was situated only yards downstream from the town bridge, the highest point of navigation on the river Usk for commercial shipping, and had been out of use for many years, until its renovation in the early 1960s.

For many years sand dredgers were a common sight in the Bristol Channel, working on the sandbanks in the Flat Holm and Steep Holm areas. The sand was sucked from the sea bed and pumped into their holds by heavy suction equipment. One such vessel, the MV *ISCA*, of 1960, one of the J. & R. Griffiths fleet, unloads her cargo at the Moderator Wharf in May 1962. The Newport Town Hall clock tower, long since demolished, dominates the skyline.

Another J. & R. Griffiths sand dredger, the steam vessel *Indium*, of 1924, passes the dock entrance as she heads upstream at the mouth of the River Usk, in October 1960.

The veteran sand dredger *Endcliffe*, of 1911, at Newport shortly before her departure for the breaker's yard at Briton Ferry, in the autumn of 1961.

The White Funnel paddle steamer *Britannia* at the Landing Stage (*above and below*), in 1955. Newport Bridge and the castle can be seen behind the steamer . On the left is Jays Furniture Shop, with its balcony, so ideally situated for watching the movements of the pleasure steamers.

The landing stage, seen here from Jays' balcony, had been used by the paddle steamers since the late nineteenth century. With the general decline in pleasure sailings in the 1950s, the White Funnel steamers ceased to call at Newport at the end of the 1956 season. The landing stage pontoons were towed to a buyer in Holland the following year.

One sailing continued to be made from Newport after 1956. That was the annual charter trip by the Harbour Commissioners. With the demise of the landing stage, the steamer berthed at the South Lock entrance. The *Bristol Queen* is seen in the lock on her return from the annual 'jaunt' on 30 June 1961.

Having disembarked the Harbour Commissioners, the *Bristol Queen* leaves Newport to return to Cardiff for her following day's sailings.

Among the least glamorous vessels to be found in any port must surely be the dredgers. Yet without their essential work of keeping the sea lanes clear, the port could not function. The mud banks of the Severn Estuary are legendary. The slimy ooze was carried into the confines of the docks by the continual movement of shipping in and out of the lock gates. The bucket dredger *Foremost IV*, of 1928, is seen in the South Dock in July 1961. The continuous line of buckets on their conveyor was adjusted to the depth of the water, so that each bucket could scoop up its quota of mud, rise out of the water and empty its contents down a chute and into the hopper alongside. In this photograph the hopper is absent, having journeyed out into the channel to empty her 'cargo' at the spoil ground, to be dispersed by the rapid tidal flow and currents.

Most of the bucket dredgers were 'dumb', that is they were not self- propelled, but were towed into position, usually by the hoppers, which were lashed alongside. However, their dredging and ancillary machinery was steam driven. The hopper, *Ebbw*, is seen in the South Dock with another load of mud for the spoil ground, in July 1961.

The two Newport hoppers, *Usk* and *Ebbw*, built by Charles Hill & Son of Bristol in 1948, were handsome ships, despite the strictly utilitarian nature of their duties. The *Usk* is seen in dry dock in the summer of 1961.

The well-proportioned bridge and wheelhouse structure would not have looked out of place on the smartest of passenger ships.

For dredging in confined areas a smaller type of dredger was equipped with a small crane, carried on the foredeck, with its own hopper amidships. The crane operator would simply lower the grab over the side, pick up the mud and drop it into the hopper. One such vessel, appropriately named *Graball*, has been at work overnight in the approach to the South Lock, and in the early morning awaits the tide to empty her spoil. In the distance the *Usk* and *Ebbw* also await the tide in the entrance channel to the dock and river mouth, the Newport Deep.

Among the most attractive vessels working in the docks were the tugs. Their sturdy, purposeful lines and bustling manoeuvrability testified to their latent power. The graceful upward sweep of the hull is shown to full advantage in this view of the Newport Screw Towing Company's *Duneagle*, berthing in the North Dock in 1960. She was built in 1943 as the *Empire Mustang* and later passed to the Tees Towing Company. where she was renamed *Dundas Cross*. On her arrival at Newport in the spring of 1958 she was renamed *Duneagle*. She was sold to Greek buyers in 1965 and was renamed *Nisos Syros*.

Another 'old-timer' was the *Dunraven*, formerly the Clyde tug, *Flying Condor*, of 1914, which arrived at Newport in 1947. In the spring of 1961 the Newport Screw Towing Company was taken over by Cory Brothers of London, who began an extensive programme of replacement of these old steam tugs with diesel vessels.

Previous page: The Newport Screw Towing Company possessed some fine 'veteran' tugs. The *Holman*, built in 1908 as the Alexandra Towing Company's *Hornby*, for service on the Mersey, arrived at Newport in 1935. She is seen entering the South Lock, shortly before being broken up at Cashmore's yard, in the spring of 1960.

While the Newport Screw Towing Company's tugs were responsible for assisting ships outside the dock, the British Transport Commission maintained tugs purely for dock work. An old member of the fleet was the *Trusty*, of 1913, seen laid up in the North Dock after being replaced by the diesel tug *St Woolos*, (below), delivered by P. K. Harris of Appledore in early 1960.

Among the many coastal cargo vessels which called regularly at Newport were the ships of Osborne & Wallis. They were used mainly for carrying coal to the company's yard in the Floating Harbour at Bristol. Their oldest ship, *Druid Stroke* of 1929, enters the South Lock in May 1962.

The Osborne & Wallis ships were named after districts in Bristol. The *Brandon*, of 1957, loads coal from one of the twenty coal hoists. At one time, every one of the hoists would be working, with ships queuing up for loading. However, by the time this photograph was taken, in August 1961, the coal trade was virtually extinct.

One of the best known landmarks in Newport is the Transporter Bridge, rearing 242 feet into the sky and spanning the River Usk at a distance of 645 feet from tower to tower. It was a masterpiece of engineering by French designer, François Amodin.

The repair yard of C. H. Bailey Ltd was always a busy place, catering for a wide variety of ships. *Above:* The *Kantamanto,* the State Yacht of the President of Ghana, undergoes an extensive refit.
Below: The coastal tanker, *Candourity,* receives attention in the spring of 1961.

Previous page: The foundation stone was laid in November 1902 and the bridge was opened on 12 September 1906. In recent years it fell into disrepair. However, it was renovated during the 1990s and once again carries passengers and vehicles across the river in its cradle. The Transporter Bridge dominates the sky-line in this early 1960s view from Belle Vue Park.

A frequent Newport visitor was the F.T. Everard tanker *Acclivity*, of 1928, seen here temporarily laid up at one of the disused coal hoists in the North Dock, in 1960.

The *Acclivity* in the South Dock, February 1962.

The *Acclivivty's* main duties were delivering fuel to the cargo vessels. Here she is bunkering the iron ore carrier, *Granada*, in the South Dock, in February 1962.

Contrasting ships in dry dock.
Above: The Newport Screw Company's tug,
Dunheron.
Left: The British Railways' cross passenger
ferry, *Falaise*.

Laid up at buoys in the South Dock for about four years was the Park-type tanker *Azure Coast*, a Liberty ship of 1944. She was eventually sold for breaking up and was towed to Vigo, in Spain, in September 1962.

At the tug berth in the North Dock. *Above:* The *Dunheron*. *Below:* The *Duneagle*, *Dunfinch* and *Dunheron*.

'Locking-out' of the 1,000ft long, 100ft wide South Lock in 1961. On the left is the coaster, *Blisworth*, while the tugs *Dunheron* and *Duneagle* prepare to assist the departure of the Blue Funnel Cargo Liner, *Polydorus*.

The *Polydorus* has left the lock and turns to starboard to enter the Newport Deep.

The Blue Funnel liner *Menestheus* arriving at Newport in February 1962.

In October 1962 Her Majesty the Queen and the Duke of Edinburgh opened the new Spencer Steelworks at Llanwern, just outside Newport. Vast amounts of iron ore then began to arrive. The ore carriers *Rio Orinoco* and *Rio Barima* called regularly from Venezuela, carrying cargoes in excess of 25,000 tons.

The Swedish steamer *Stallberg* in the South Dock, April 1962.

The Holland America Line's *Akkrumdyk* silhouetted against the setting sun, in February 1961.

Two
Cardiff and Penarth

The entrances to three of the Cardiff docks, the East and West Bute and the Roath, were approached by a stretch of water known as the 'Drain', which culminated at the Pier Head. The pleasure steamers used the pontoons to embark their passengers and frequently shared their berths with the tugs. In this view, taken on 13 March 1963, the motor vessel *St Trillo*, newly purchased by P. & A. Campbell Ltd from the Liverpool and North Wales Steam Packet Co. Ltd., lies opposite the tug *Royal Rose*.

The BP tanker, *British Guardian*, is towed into the Roath Basin while the paddle steamer, *Cardiff Queen*, approaches the Pier Head, during the summer of 1964.

Previous page: Ships unloading their cargoes in the Queen Alexandra Dock, Cardiff, in the summer of 1964.

In the foreground is Penarth Dock Basin before it became the Marina, and beyond is Cardiff Bay before the barrage. The *Cardiff Queen* passes the entrance to the Queen Alexandra Dock as she leaves the Drain, on her way from Cardiff to Penarth and Weston-Super-Mare, in 1961.

The north end of Penarth Dock in 1961. On the pontoon is the Fishguard to Rosslare passenger ferry *St Patrick* undergoing her annual refit. On the left is the grab dredger *Mudeford* and on the right is the Bristol Channel's oldest dredger, *Peeress*, dating from 1920.

On the evening of 30 March 1961 the hull of the tug *Cardiff Rose* was holed by the propeller of the Norwegian tanker, *Harwi*. The tug was immediately beached near the Pier Head and became almost submerged at high tide. All her crew escaped injury.

On the day following her accident the *Cardiff Rose* lies high and dry on the mud, at low tide. An inspection of her hull revealed extensive damage and she was subsequently broken up.

The *Cardiff Queen* makes her way up the Drain into Cardiff, on 17 September 1960.

The *Bristol Queen* arriving at the Pier Head on 10 June 1965.

The dredger *Peeress* in the Drain, awaiting the tide and the return of her hopper in 1964.

Affectionately known as the 'Ernie P' the hopper *Sir Ernest Palmer* waits in the Drain to manoeuvre alongside the dredger *Foremost IV*, to load another cargo of Bristol Channel mud for the spoil ground in 1965.

Previous page: The *Cardiff Queen* at the Pier Head on the morning of 20 May 1961.

The *Foremost IV* at work in the Drain in 1965.

The hopper *GWR 2* leaving the Queen Alexandra Dock in 1965.

The tugs *Plumgarth* and *Westgarth* at work in the Roath Dock in 1964.

The *Exegarth*, one of the four tugs needed to guide the Shell tanker, *Harpula*, through the docks in 1964.

The Blue Funnel cargo liner *Hector* in the Queen Alexandra Dock in 1965. The Blue Funnel vessels were particularly handsome ships, most of which were named after characters in Greek mythology.

The Strick Line cargo vessel *Turkistan* in the Queen Alexandra Dock in 1965.

Previous page: The *Harpula* leaving the Roath Dock and entering the basin to proceed to sea. All of the Shell tankers were given the Latin names of shells.

On a warm summer evening in 1964 the Finnish steamship *Ragni Paulin* waits to unload her cargo of timber in the Queen Alexandra Dock.

The Scarweather light-vessel undergoing an overhaul in the Mountstuart Dry Dock in March 1966. Her normal station marked the western extremity of the Scarweather Sands, in Swansea Bay.

The light-vessel was sharing the dry dock with the P. & A. Campbell motor-vessel, *Westward Ho*, which had been acquired, in the autumn of 1965, from the Red Funnel Line of Southampton.

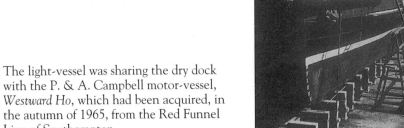

There were two Mountstuart Dry Docks, side by side, situated close to the Pier Head. In the No.2 Dry Dock, a British Rail ferry receives attention.

With their overhauls complete, the Scarweather light-vessel and the *Westward Ho* lie in the Roath Basin awaiting the return to their duties.

The entrance lock to the Queen Alexandra Dock was drained during the mid-1960s for extensive maintenance. While the work was in progress ships used the Roath Basin entrance.

The veteran White Funnel steamer *Glen Usk*, of 1914, laid up in the East Bute Dock early in 1963. She was towed to Passage West, Cork, for breaking up on 29 April the same year.

The *Bristol Queen* and *Cardiff Queen* at their winter quarters in the Queen Alexandra Dock, in October 1963.

The *Cardiff Queen* passes the hopper *Sir Ernest Palmer* on her approach to the Pier Head, in May 1965. The boatmen are waiting to take the steamer's stern rope to a bollard on the quay, adjacent to her berth. On her departure this rope will be used to pull her around to face seaward.

Previous page: The sand dredger *Isabel* in the West Bute Basin, in the early 1960s.

The former Plymouth passenger liner tender *Sir Richard Grenville*, was purchased in March 1964, by Jersey Lines Ltd, for service between the Channel Islands and St Malo, under the name *La Duchesse De Normandie*. She visited Cardiff on several occasions for overhaul and is seen here in the East Bute Dock Basin in March 1965.

With Penarth in the background, the coaster *Kylebank* leaves the Queen Alexandra Lock in 1965.

The sand dredger *Dunkerton* unloads her cargo in the Roath Basin in 1965.

The sand dredger *Bowpride* in dry dock; a vessel of 1,000 tons capacity, built in Holland for F. Bowles & Sons Ltd, in service from April 1960.

The tug *Exegarth* towing the German motor-vessel *Brunswick into Cardiff in 1963*.

The tugs *Westgarth* (left) and *Tregarth* towing the cargo vessel *Landwade* past the imposing promontory of Penarth Head on their way into Cardiff, 1964.

The F. T. Everard tanker *Anteriority* discharging her cargo at Ely Harbour in 1960. The harbour consisted of a number of wharves on the River Ely alongside Penarth Dock. Coal hoists were originally situated here but were later replaced by an oil and petrol storage depot.

The *Anteriority* passing Penarth Head on her departure from Ely Harbour in 1960.

The *Cardiff Queen* (left), and *Bristol Queen* laid up in Penarth Dock at the end of the 1960 season.

Penarth Dock in May 1961, with the grab dredger, *Mudeford*, (right), and the *Glen Usk*.

The Dutch motor-vessel *Amstelstroom* in Cardiff Roads, 1961.

The Houlder Bros iron ore carrier *Oreosa* in Cardiff Roads, 1964.

The Blue Star liner *Brisbane Star* heads out to sea from Cardiff in the summer of 1963.

Three
Barry and the Bristol Channel Pilots

The tug *Royal Falcon* in the entrance lock to Barry Docks in March 1960.

Previous page: Barry was the base for the pilots of the 'up-channel' ports of the Severn Estuary. The pilots would board the in-bound ships, and be 'picked out' from those outward bound, in Barry Roads. The Newport steam pilot cutter, *Belle Usk*, is seen off Barry in August 1955. She ran aground on Nell's Point, Barry, in December 1957 and became a total loss.

The tug *Exegarth* assists with the docking of the tanker *Regent Caribou* at Barry in 1962.

Further tanker arrivals at Barry in 1962. *Above:* The *Cerinthus, below:* the *Border Fusilier*.

The *Welsh Rose* leaving Barry Harbour on a blustery day in January 1961.

The *Welsh Rose* again, towing a ship out of Barry in May 1962.

The *Bristol Queen* arriving at Barry Pier in 1963. The dredging of the approach to the pier gave the steamers the advantage of being able to berth at low water, as seen here.

The *Cardiff Queen* at Barry Pier in 1964.

The tugs *Caroline Davies* (left), and *St. Baruch* entering the dock with a tanker in tow, March 1960. The former had a chequered career; she was built at Dumbarton in 1909, as the *J.O. Gravel* and was employed by her Canadian owners in salvage work in the St. Lawrence River. She returned to

Great Britain in 1921 and performed duties on the Manchester Ship Canal as the *Clarendon*, before her purchase, in 1952, by J. Davies Towage & Salvage Ltd. of Cardiff. She worked in the Bristol Channel ports as the *Caroline Davies* until she was broken up at Passage West, Cork in 1962.

Following the loss of the steam cutter *Belle Usk* in December 1957, the Newport Pilotage Authority took delivery of the diesel cutter *Alpha II* from J. Tyrell of Arklow in early 1958. At the same time the old Barry Pier railway station building was converted into a lodge for the Newport pilots. Previously they had been accommodated aboard the larger steam cutters. The *Alpha II* is seen off Barry in 1962.

The *Alpha II* at Barry Pier, May 1962. She had been named after a former sailing cutter, hence the suffix 'II'.

A second diesel cutter, *Spencer*, also built by J. Tyrell, began service in December 1959. She is seen entering Barry Harbour in March 1962.

The pilot cutters were tough little vessels which had to put to sea in the worst of weathers. Here, the *Spencer* heads out of Barry in sea conditions usually described by the pilot apprentices as 'a bit of a lop'.

The Barry pilot cutter *Quest* in Barry Harbour in May 1962.

The Bristol pilot cutter *Queen Mother*, off Barry in the summer of 1962.

The *Queen Mother* and *Alpha II* in Barry Harbour in 1962.

The Cardiff pilot cutter *Warren Evans* in the Bute East Dock, Cardiff, in 1962. She is undergoing repairs to her port bow, which had been badly damaged in heavy weather alongside a cargo ship, while taking off a pilot in Barry Roads, an occupational hazard for the pilot cutters.

The coaster, *Anthony M*, has just boarded her pilot and heads up channel for Newport in March 1962. The deck of a pilot cutter was an ideal vantage point from which to photograph the ships which passed through Barry Roads. On the following pages are some of the vessels seen in the Bristol Channel early in 1962.

The veteran steamer *Jan*, bound for Newport with a cargo of pit props from Scandinavia.

The ore carrier *Atlantic Faith*.

The Blue Funnel liner *Dolius*.

The Avenue Shipping Company's motor-vessel *Antrim*, launched at Glasgow in January 1962, bound for Newport on her maiden voyage.

The Finnish motor-vessel *Triton*.

In April 1962 the steamship *Hoyle* arrived in Barry Roads. She was built in 1935 as a dredger for the Mersey Docks and Harbour Board, and had been purchased by the Cardiff company Davies, Middleton and Davies.

After various alterations the *Hoyle* began work as a sand dredger, suitably renamed *Sand Galore*. Her first cargo of 3,000 tons of sand was the largest single sand cargo to be landed at Cardiff.

Four
Towards West Wales

*Left and below:*Early on a Sunday morning, in June 1960, the fishing vessel *Altmark* was driven ashore in high winds, near Sker Point, Porthcawl, after an engine failure. Her crew escaped injury, but several attempts to re-float the vessel were unsuccessful and she became a total loss.

Previous page: The Harrison cargo liner *Administrator* in the King's Dock, Swansea, in 1963.

The Swansea pilot cutter *Seamark* in Swansea Bay. She had been built by P K. Harris of Appledore, Devon, and was launched in April 1959. She replaced the last of the Swansea steam cutters, the thirty-six year old *Roger Beck*, in December 1959.

The *Seamark* moored alongside the *Bristol Queen* at Pockett's Wharf, on the bank of the River Tawe, at Swansea in 1965. The wharf was named after the Pockett family, who played a prominent part in the development of Swansea's coastal cargo trade and the regular passenger packet service between Swansea and North Devon.

The tugs *Murton*, of 1929, and *Herculaneum*, of 1909, in Swansea Docks. September 1961.

The tugs *Clyneforth* and *Wallasey* in the Kings Dock, Swansea, in 1963.

The Irish coaster *Ballyhill* in the Prince of Wales Dock, Swansea, in 1963.

The Brocklebank liner, *Martand*, a regular trader to Indian ports, in the Kings Dock, Swansea. 1963.

The Scandinavian steamer *Ivar* unloading pit props, in 1963.

The Danish motor-vessel, *Grete Skou*, in the King's Dock, 1963.

The cargo steamer *Kalliopi* at Swansea, in 1963.

The P. & A. Campbell paddle steamer *Glen Gower* was a frequent visitor to Swansea during the course of her thirty-five year career. She was broken up in 1960, but her name was perpetuated by a Swansea sand dredger, seen here in the South Dock, now the Swansea Marina, in the early 1960s.

The 'business end' of the Swansea dredger *Abertawe*, showing the driving mechanism and conveyor which wound the buckets in and out of the murky depths. Who can forget the 'clunk, splosh' as each bucket emptied its contents down the chute into the hopper alongside?

In 1962 P. & A. Campbell Ltd. revived one of their occasional pre-war day trips. On 24 May the *Bristol Queen* sailed from Cardiff and Ilfracombe on a return journey to Milford Haven. Here, the Milford Haven pilot cutter approaches and the pilot waits to board the paddle steamer.

The journey to and from the dock entrance was full of interest. During the early 1960s Milford Haven was transformed into one of the country's major oil importing depots and numerous oil tankers were seen. Here, the Norwegian owned *Davanger* unloads her cargo at one of the terminals.

Looking somewhat out of place among her larger and more modern consorts, the *Esso Chelsea*, dating from 1945, approaches her berth.

At anchor near the Milford Haven Dock entrance was the ocean-going salvage tug *Turmoil*. She had featured prominently in the headlines in 1952 when she towed the stricken Norwegian cargo vessel *Flying Enterprise* through heavy seas in the English Channel towards Falmouth. Her master, Capt. Henrik Carlsen, remained alone on his ship, which, despite the efforts of the *Turmoil*, sank when only fifty miles from the Cornish coast.

STELLA

TRINITY HOUSE

LONDON

96

Five

Trinity House

The island of Lundy stands like a sentinel at the entrance to the Bristol Channel, ten and a half nautical miles from Hartland Point, its nearest headland on the North Devon Coast. Trinity House built the first lighthouse on Lundy in 1819. Unfortunately, the site chosen, the highest point of the island, was frequently shrouded in low cloud which obscured the light. It fell into disuse in the 1890s, when two new lighthouses were built at lower levels on the north and south ends of the island. In this view of Lundy, the north lighthouse can be seen, as well as the rugged west coast, with its granite cliffs exposed to the full fury of the Atlantic gales.

Previous page: The tender *Stella* at the Bristol Channel depot of Trinity House in the King's Dock, Swansea, in 1963.

The administration of the lighthouses, buoys and beacons around the coasts of England and Wales is the responsibility of the Corporation of Trinity House. Depots were established at various ports, and a fleet of vessels regularly visited the beacons in their allotted areas for inspection and maintenance. The Trinity House tender, *Alert*, is seen off Lundy in 1961, during an inspection of the north and south lighthouses. On her foredeck are a number of buoys which, having been serviced ashore, will now be returned to their positions.

A Bristol Channel light-vessel undergoing maintenance at Swansea. During her period in dock a replacement vessel would be marking her position off the Pembrokeshire coast, approximately seventeen nautical miles south-west of Tenby.

The Breaksea light-vessel in position a few miles south of Barry, on a blustery afternoon in 1962.

As night descends over the Bristol Channel the sea-lights mark the hazards of this most dangerous seaway. The Breaksea light-vessel flashes her warning light only a short distance off shore but, as one of her crew of four men on his four week turn of duty once said, 'the distance might as well be a hundred miles!'

On a Sunday afternoon in 1963 the paddle steamer *Cardiff Queen*, made the crossing from Ilfracombe to Lundy in gale force winds and very heavy seas. In Bideford Bay, two indistinct shapes were seen off the port bow, which, in a brief easing of the torrential rain, resolved into the Trinity House tender *Stella*, with the Breaksea light-vessel in tow. The ships were bound for Falmouth, where the light-vessel was to undergo a major overhaul, but in view of the weather conditions, they were heading for the lee of Lundy for shelter.

The Trinity House vessel *Patricia*, at anchor in Cardiff Roads in 1964, during a tour of inspection of the Bristol Channel beacons by the Elder Brethren of Trinity House.

Six

Across the Channel

The riverside wharves of Barnstaple, on the River Taw, and Bideford, on the River Torridge, were frequently used by small coastal cargo vessels. The coaster, *Michael* M, passes the sand dunes of Braunton Burrows, as she leaves the estuary of the two rivers in 1963.

A coaster heads out of the River Torridge and westward into the sunset. The promontory on the horizon is Hartland Point, the tide-riven headland at the southern extremity of the encircling arms of Bideford Bay.

Previous page: The Bristol Queen at anchor off Lundy, 15 May 1963. Here, as at the north Devon villages of Lynmouth and Clovelly, the steamer passengers were ferried ashore in small boats.

The *Stan Woolaway*, built in 1955, leaving Ilfracombe in 1962. She was a sand dredger which frequently worked the sandbanks near the Holms, and landed her cargo in the harbour of the north Devon resort. On one such journey, returning with a full load of sand, she capsized and sank between Lynmouth and Ilfracombe.

The *Cardiff Queen* at Ilfracombe Pier, 17 July 1966. The opening of the pier in 1873 transformed Ilfracombe from a quiet fishing village into a major holiday resort, as it became the destination of an increasing number of pleasure steamers.

The coastal minesweeper HMS *St David*, part of the Bristol Channel Royal Naval Reserve, at anchor off Ilfracombe, in 1963.

These photographs were taken from the *Bristol Queen* on her departure, stern first, from the pier. The *Bristol Queen's* master, Capt. Jack George, was a consummate ship handler, who ensured that his passengers were treated to a close-up view of the *St David*.

Seven
Avonmouth and Bristol

On this, and the previous page, the liner *Kungsholm*, (21,141 gross tons) is shown at her anchorage near Clevedon, in May 1965.

Previous page: For some years during the 1960s the Swedish American Line scheduled visits to the Bristol Channel as part of its Springtime Cruises. The vessels anchored in Walton Bay, where the passengers were trans-shipped to one of the P. & A. Campbell steamers, which landed them at Avonmouth. Coaches waited for them at the dockside, which took them on tours of the local countryside, visiting castles, stately homes and gardens.

The *Bristol Queen* approaches the *Kungsholm* to return her passengers after their day ashore, on 5 May 1965.

The *Kungsholm*, on her departure from the Bristol Channel, meets an oil tanker bound for Avonmouth.

The tug *Sea Queen* tows the Norwegian oil tanker *Simona* out of Avonmouth in May 1965.

The docks at Avonmouth possessed extensive oil and petrol storage tanks, cold stores, granaries and fruit stores. The Fyffe Line's *Chuscal* approaches Portishead, outward bound for the West Indies and another cargo of bananas, in 1964.

The motor-vessel *Fruin* leaving Avonmouth with a deck cargo of cars for Belfast. The chimneys of the Portishead Power Station, once a familiar landmark but long since demolished, stand behind the woods.

One of the most unusual vessels in the Channel was the Port of Bristol Authority's combined bucket dredger and hopper. She was unnamed and referred to simply as *BD10* (BD denoting Bristol Docks). The buckets were lowered and raised on a continuous conveyor through her stern, and were emptied into the hopper amidships on their way around. She is shown at Avonmouth in 1965.

On her way up the River Avon in 1965 the coaster *Shetland Trader* passes the ferry which crosses the river between the village of Pill, (from where this photograph was taken), and Shirehampton, on the Gloucestershire bank.

A coastal minesweeper journeys up the Avon on a courtesy visit to Bristol, in 1964.

The Polish steamer, *Wrocław*, passing the *Bristol Queen* in Sea Mills Reach. The restricted waterway meant that there was little room for errors of navigation.

The journey up and down the River Avon, to and from the Bristol City Docks, was fraught with hazards. In this 1965 view, the Bristol Steam Navigation Company's *Apollo* negotiates the river's most dangerous part, the Horseshoe Bend.

The grab dredger, *BD Clifton*, approaches the bend on her journey upstream. The bend could only be negotiated safely within one-and-a-half hours either side of high water. Outside that slack water period, ships ran a grave risk of being swept on to the mud by the fast flowing tides.

With the Bristol suburb of Sea Mills in the background, the *BD Clifton* continues her journey, passing the outward bound sand dredger, *Steep Holm*.

The steam sand dredger *Steep Holm*, built in 1950, has just passed under the Clifton Suspension Bridge on her way out to the channel, in 1964. The vessel met an untimely end in October 1968 when she ran aground on Tusker Rock, Porthcawl, and defied all attempts at salvage.

The *Camerton* in the River Avon, 1964. Following the loss of the *Steep Holm*, the *Camerton* became the last steam sand dredger in the Bristol Channel.

On a Sunday morning in the summer of 1963 the tug *Salisbury* hurries down the Avon Gorge to meet an inward bound ship. A local yachtsman has 'hitched' a tow.

The tug *Kingsgarth* passing the Port of Bristol Authority's signal station at Shirehampton, on the Gloucestershire bank of the River Avon, in 1963. The lookout, with the aid of a microphone, hailed each ship that passed to inform her master of traffic movements in the river. The *Kingsgarth* came to an unfortunate end, in March of the following year, when she sank after colliding with the cargo liner *Port Launceston*, off Avonmouth.

JOHN KING

A Bristol Channel sunset, seen from the deck of the *Bristol Queen* on 5 May 1965, as she steams back to Cardiff having completed her tendering duties for the passenger liner, *Kungsholm*. The liner has weighed anchor and is heading out to sea. In the distance, just ahead of her bow, the English & Welsh Grounds light-vessel is about to begin her nightly vigil; warning ships to steer clear of the extensive mud banks in mid-channel. The city of Cardiff stands in the path of the sunlight on the far coast.

Previous page: On a hazy morning in May 1964 the tug *John King* assists the Finnish motor-vessel *Thorkill Lund* on the tortuous passage up river to Bristol.